Our Move to the Woods

Dan England

ISBN: 978-1-887048-20-0

The painting on the front cover of our cabin in the woods is by Carole Cochran.

Published by
Greenfield Center Press
Crossville, TN 38558

gcpress@aol.com

Printed in the United States of America

Introduction

My wife, Donna and I left the corporate world and moved to the woods. The "why" of the move is covered in a previous book we co-authored titled, How to Retire Before 50, and my book titled, Miracles Do Happen. I won't go into the reason we left our jobs other that to say that we were fed up with the corporate world and the rat race of life outside the woods. Earlier I wrote a book titled Welcome to the Real Corporate World: Surviving and Succeeding in a Large Corporation. It was written like a last gasp before I left the office as well as a warning to the young people about the pitfalls of office politics.

That all being said, this book looks at some of our experiences in the woods. Many were humorous (at least to us) and sometimes not so humorous at the time. However, as I grow older I have reframed these experiences as an important part of my life that have a positive outcome.

I hope you, the reader, will enjoy the stories and just maybe help you reframe some of your "wilderness" experiences. In any event, even if only a single copy of the book makes it into print, re-reading it over and over in the old folks home (if I am so lucky) will help pass the time. By that time I will probably think the stories are about someone else.

Donna and I watched the movie "The Notebook" and promised each other that we will read our books to the other if one is incapable of reading.

It is my intention to tell these stories in a chronological order as we progressed deeper into the woods and then out of the woods. Donna is helping me with this and is refreshing my memory. God Bless good wives!

Before I start, I'll give you a little background. Our adventure started in Illinois where Donna and I had good corporate jobs. Our first move was to New York State for jobs with the same company. We "retired" from our jobs in New York and escaped to the woods in Missouri.

Now, join us on our journey in the woods.

I

Chapter 1 - The Beginning

We finally did it. We broke from our corporate masters in New York State in 1995: finally free! But our real adventure didn't start until a year later. We planned to move south but decided to wait until our youngest graduated from high school and headed to college.

In the intervening year, we shed three of our four vehicles, bought a motorhome and a cabin in Missouri on top of a mountain that set on our very own 37 acres. We named our place Highland Acres. I tell that tale in my book Miracles Do Happen!

It took several trips to move our things from New York State to Missouri. On our final trip south we crammed most of the remaining things we owned into a rental truck. We loaded our red pickup truck with personal things - even our plants - and headed to the woods.

After unloading our truck in Missouri with the help of local friends we made in the past year, we began settling into our new cabin. Our realtor Don told us that the previous owner had some trouble with the locals. He bought up much of the property at the top of the mountain (our 37 acres was the middle of his two 40 acres) and considered the dirt road in front of his cabin (now ours), as part of his domain. Hence, he strung barbed wire across the road - in effect closing it. Don told us that one night unhappy neighbors took the border fence down and took a shot at the cabin as a warning. He showed us a hole in the glass of the front door to prove his story as true.

Don also recommended we never lock the door of our cabin when we leave the property. The reason being that locals liked to come in to a house purchased by strangers and snoop around to be sure they were not government agents.

Now, I'm not sure that Don wasn't playing around with us city slickers in his story but we were a bit apprehensive anyway. Weeks passed as we gradually unpacked our boxes and became more familiar with our new surroundings. However, we hadn't met anyone new. Our nearest neighbor was over a mile away. All seemed peaceful.

Then one night, terror struck!

This is how it went: We worked all day unpacking and doing yard work and we were exhausted. At the end of the day we climbed up the stairway to our loft and settled down for the night. We fell into a deep sleep. With no street lights or illuminated signs, the woods were a very, very dark place indeed. Also, there was almost complete silence. Occasionally, some insect or bug would squeak. Oh yes, Donna reminded me that infrequently an owl hooted or screeched. I loved that part of being in the woods.

Suddenly, there was a sharp violent bang/boom and then a clatter that sounded like shattering glass. Fearfully, we awoke and I shouted, "*What the hell was that*!". Our first thought was that we were under shotgun attack by the woods people Don warned us about. Oh, no! I looked at the clock and it was 3 AM.

I carefully rolled out of bed and tried to quietly drop on the floor but instead hit the floor with a loud thud. (When we first purchased the property we bought an antique iron bed that was much taller than modern beds.) In the blackness I slithered along the wood planked floor like a snake. Donna whispered,"*Where are you*?"

As I "snaked" my way over the loft floor I felt the pain of slivers of wood penetrating my chest. I slithered to the wooded stairway and slinked down the steps to the open great room.

I made it to the middle window of the room, popped my head up and peered into the darkness. Nothing! Then, gaining some confidence I crawled, now on my knees, to the other window and to the door and found no broken glass.

Donna told me she whispered my name and there was no response. Her heart pounded and she didn't know whether to roll out of bed, under the bed, or toward the stairs. She still felt a threat.

Satisfied that we "probably" weren't under attack, I walked up the stairs, crouching this time, and said, "*I think it's all clear*." Then bravely, I flipped on the light switch.

"*Oops*,," I said. I saw the PVC pipe that I just installed laying on the floor along the entire width of the loft by our bed. The clothes we earlier loaded on hangers on the PCV pipe were now all setting in a big heap. We couldn't stop laughing!

Chapter 2 - You Moved Where?

Our property was located on a dirt road in the mountains in a very remote area of Southern Missouri. We had to drive several miles on the dirt road down the mountain to get to the highway. Once on the highway, we had to drive another six or seven miles to a very small town that had a population of less than three hundred people to get our mail.

The town had one gas station, a small grocery store and an old chicken restaurant that held less 10 people. The closest McDonald's and movie theater were 45 miles away and the movie theatre only had one screen. The closest mall was over ninety miles away. It took months to meet our closest neighbor who live a far piece down the road. I could go on but I think you get the picture.

After we got settled, we started ordering things we needed by mail. We ordered several magazines from a company that would give you millions of dollars if your were lucky enough in their drawing. (They didn't say how often they drew.)

We waited a few weeks anticipating some good reading material coming in the mail. In one mail delivery, a letter came from the magazine company. Donna opened it and came running to show me what they said. "*Did we win a million bucks*?", I asked. "*Probably not,*" Donna said. She was laughing hysterically. She read the letter to me:

> "*We are sorry, we don't deliver to third world countries.*"

We found out early how deep we moved into the woods. We also learned about living with wild animals.

Chapter 3 - The Squirrel Sagas

This is the tale of how squirrels impacted our move to the woods. However, it all started one day years before we actually made the move.

The Omen

Donna and I were the owners of a campground membership in the same county where we eventually moved. The campground was huge: Five Square miles - bigger than several countries. It was called a ranch complete with five camping areas and five storage areas where trailers, 5th wheels, motorhomes, 4 wheelers and other camping toys could be stored for free. We loved going to the ranch! It had two pools, tennis courts, a clubhouse, a restaurant and a winding stream that ran through it that even had a waterfall. Donna and I often talked about leaving our jobs and moving to the ranch full times which many other had done.

The ranch also had many roads. You had to drive almost three miles on a paved road before you even got to the gatehouse. One day as we were arriving at the "ranch" for a mini-vacation we were driving on this road. Our kids were with us. As we were driving over the winding road a squirrel jumped out in front of us. My son Rob screamed, "*Dad, look out, there is a squirrel on the road.*" When I took driver's education back in the 1960s we were taught to never ever swerve to miss a live animal that was on the road. The reason being that you might crash into another car, a tree or something else while most animals will scamper around. Predicting where they will be is almost impossible. The recommendation from our teacher was to keep your cool and keep driving. He recommended slowing down a bit as long as there was not a car close behind you.

So..... As the squirrel ran in circles, I kept on driving. Soon everyone in the car, except me, was screaming for me to miss the squirrel. Splat!!! We heard a thud and felt a bump. Looking back we saw the squirrel flat as a pancake on the road, except for his or her tail still flapping in the wind. Rob, being an animal lover yelled, "*Dad, you murdered the squirrel.*" Then a chorus of accusations arose from others. Nothing I said in my defense could absolve me. Apparently they thought I should have hit a tree.

Through the years the story of me, murdering the squirrel, became family lore. One Christmas Rob bought me a large plaster squirrel. It had had a chunk out one of the paws. He said he bought a defective one that would forev-

er remind me of my evil deed. It still sits in a place of honor on the hearth of the fireplace in our family room. I had a history that would haunt me.

There's more. Stay tuned!

The Attack - They Almost Ate the Whole Thing

Now fast forward in time to a scary squirrel story from when we moved to the woods.

After a few months we started to notice chips of wood on the deck. We looked around to see where they were coming from. We looked up at the roof line and saw an area that looked like something had chewed on it. As days went on we could see more evidence in other areas of our home where our cabin had been chewed on. We also often heard a chewing sound in the attic at night.

One day we heard the chewing on the back deck coming from an area just under the roof line. I peered into the opening where the sound came from. Oh no! Two small beady red eyes were looking at me. Then as my vision cleared I saw the culprit: A scrawny grey squirrel and I swear he barred his teeth at me. Donna looked in and saw the critter too.

The attack got worse and every day and we saw evidence that our cabin was being eaten. What to do?

The Defense

We called our realtor Don to get some advice. We told him our sorrows and he, with no hesitation, told us what was happening: *"The woods around you are over populated with squirrels. There isn't enough for them to eat so many had taken to eating houses."* I said, *"You've got to be kidding!"*

Don assured us this was a common problem. "*What are we supposed to do?*", Donna asked. Then Don laid out a solution to the war the squirrels had made on our house.

> *"The best way to stop this is with cayenne pepper. Squirrels can't stand it. What people do is put it in paint and paint the mixture on the house. Add one can of the pepper for every gallon of paint."*

We were skeptical but also desperate, so we headed to the local hardware store and bought enough paint to cover the cabin and then to the grocery store and bought all the cayenne pepper they had. Then Donna and I mixed up the brew. With the help of a friend we did what Don recommended and turned up the heat on our cabin.

Miraculously it worked!!! The attacks and chewing stopped. We were elated!

We proudly told our family about the attack and how we stopped it. But when my son Rob heard the story he warned us:

"Dad, remember you murdered a squirrel on the road? Their kin are getting revenge. This is not going to end. It's squirrel Karma."

Oh, dear! I hoped he was wrong.

As I said, the chewing on the house stopped, but my son was right. It was not over. The squirrels then decided to bedevil us by moving into our attic. Every night we heard the noises being made by the squirrel family. You could hear their claws scratching on the ceiling of the kitchen. They had fun running around all night keeping us awake.

Another evidence that war was not over was when Donna strung little white lights around the edge of the front porch roof. She enjoyed seeing them all lit up at night all year round. One morning she came down the stairs from our loft and looked out the front window and saw two squirrels climbing on the lights and gnawing on the wires. Then, Donna got really, really mad. She knew that the defense had to turn to a counter attack. She decided to take up arms.

The Counter Attack - Target Practice

We headed for the local hardware store and bought a BB gun and plenty of BBs. Then we set a target in the back yard and started practicing. Donna became a pretty good shot. After the practice we decided to go on the attack. Donna was especially determined to win the squirrel war once and for all.

One time she spotted an enemy squirrel on the ground coming near our cabin. He looked over and saw Donna with her BB gun raised. With the squirrel instinct of danger he scampered up the nearest tall tree safely out of range.

As he reacher the top of the tree and climbed out on a branch he dropped like a rock to the ground. He hit the ground, bounced, then scattered off. He probably lost his balance. The encroachments on our property seemed to slow down as we stood watch with the BB gun, but the nighttime scratching didn't end. The reserves had to be called in.

Reinforcements: Donna's Family to the Rescue

Donna's dad was a woodsman. So was her brother-in-law. They were hunters. Donna told me how when she was a child many meals came from the woods - mostly from rabbits and squirrels. So the family came to visit us and the men were armed. The first thing Donna's dad and her brother-in-law did after they arrived was go get hunting and fishing licenses.

After a couple of days the feasts began - plenty of fish and mounds of squirrels. We could hear the boom, boom of guns in the woods for days. The men would clean the animals and Donna's mom would prepare them for cooking. There was a pile of the squirrels - the harvest - not sure how many fish.

The Feast

The night before the family left for home our dining room table was set and the centerpiece was a big serving plate with a pile on it of what looked like very small chickens. The big plate was surrounded with many other smaller serving plates and bowls filled with all kinds of vegetables. There was a big bowl of mashed potatoes and a bowl of what I assumed was squirrel gravy.

I looked on in wonder. Then Donna and her family started piling the feast on their plates. They grabbed the chicken like things and started chewing on them as if they were ears of corn. I sat still and just watched. I lost my appetite!

Peace - At Last

The squirrel irritations stopped. I guess the little pests that were still left moved on to a more compliant territory. We finally settled peacefully in our cabin in the woods. We met some nice neighbors, found a good church and loved exploring our property. However, at times life could be challenging. Following are a couple of chapters that will give you an overview of where we lived.

Chapter 4 - Life in the Mountains and Trees

Our 37 acres was set among the trees in the Ozark Mountains of Southern Missouri near the border with Arkansas. It also was close to several lakes - Bull Shoals Lake being the closest. The White River of Bill Clinton's impeachment fame ran a few miles from our mountain. There were no cornfields or other crops being grown. But there were plenty of rocks all around.

We named our property Highland Acres. Life was fun but sometimes challenging. Following are some stories that marked our time at Highland Acres.

Our cabin was on top of a mountain and we knew that a valley and other mountains were off in the distance - but we couldn't see them. Donna was not happy about that and spoke about her unhappiness often. One thing I learned about Donna is that when she "speaks" things happen.

Donna invited her cousin Gloria, her husband Larry and their son to visit. Larry's major in college was forestry (Larry and Gloria visited us in the woods previously). Donna wanted a view and asked Larry to take down a few trees.

Since I love trees, I objected to the plan. Donna said she only wanted a few trees cut down so I reluctantly relented. Little did I know that the there was more danger to our trees coming. I'll tell you more of that later.

I remember standing on the deck right off our loft bedroom and watching trees fall, one by one. Donna gave instructions to Larry by walkie talkie as he moved from tree to tree. As trees fell, a view appeared of the valley and mountains off in the horizon. After that, Larry and his son sawed up the fallen trees and we had plenty of firewood for the coming winter.

While Larry was in the forrest taking down trees he found many copperhead snakes that we didn't know were there. He told us he took care of them (I guess he moved them). Larry was Donna's hero.

We were learning how to live in the woods and mountains, but sometimes we missed the things we enjoyed in more civilized areas. So once in a while we took trips away from the mountains.

Chapter 5 - Trips to Civilization

Our Trip to the Movies

One of the first trips out of the woods was when we ventured to a small city (more than 50 miles away) that had a movie theater. It only had one screen but that was fine since we didn't even have one screen where we lived.

We settled in our seats eagerly waiting for the movie to start. It had been many months since we had been to the movies back in Illinois. The theatre was crowded and it was very hot inside. Suddenly, the manager rushed into the theatre and told us the air conditioner broke down. We had to leave, disappointed - with a refund. That was our one and only trip to the movies!

We tried to escape the woods at least once a month. Our favorite designations were Branson and Springfield.

Branson

Branson was fun and only 50 miles away. The road to Branson had many twists and turns. I got carsick every time we went there. Even today when I think about those trips I started to get nauseated

Branson has a population of only 10,520 people but it is one of the most visited vacation designations in the United States. You could watch shows given by famous entertainers like Andy Williams, The Lennon Sister and Wayne Newton. There were other attractions like Silver Dollar City and Dolly Pardon's Dixie Stampede. (The "Dixie" was taken out of the name recently about the same time the Dixie Chicks became the "Chicks".) One time before we actually moved we met the owners of Silver Dollar City at a church in Branson. They were very gracious and welcoming. It was the first time I ever met billionaires.

One special time our Illinois family visited and we all travelled to Branson. Donna and I had a great time showing them around town. For me, the most fun and best memory was the family taking a ride in a "Duck" on the streets and in the water.

Ducks were first hatched by General Motors durning World War II for the purpose of getting soldiers, artillery and supplies ashore during landings

on beaches during combat. These small sturdy boats even had wheels so the Duck could run on the beaches and roads. Their use was essential to victory. In March 1945, the Allies used the Ducks to cross the Rhine River into Germany which sealed the fate of Hitler and the Nazis. After the war, thousand of Ducks were retired and eventually many ended up as tourist attractions.

We eagerly bought tickets for a Duck voyage and climbed on board. We travelled through the streets of Branson as the "Captain", over a loudspeaker, told us about the Duck, what we were seeing and what we would be doing on our voyage. We finally splashed into Lake Taneycomo. After paddling around for a while, the Captain asked for a volunteer to be a temporary Captain. My granddaughter Anissa, age 5, eagerly shot up her hand. She bravely marched up front and took the helm. We were elated. Our fellow crew mates laughed and clapped. Anissa was given a Duck whistle (she recently told me she still had it). I will never forget that memory. After that voyage, as we were again on dry land in our land vehicle, we saw William Golden, one of the Oak Ridge Boys (the one with the long beard) walking down Main Street: a special treat!

Another time in Branson Donna and I met Charlie, Anita Bryant's husband, at a gas station. He was driving a huge vintage Cadillac with an emblem on the hood of a bucking bronco. He gave us free tickets to Anita's theatre to watch her birthday celebration. So we went to the show.

We sat right up very near the front in Anita's theatre. There was a couple in front of us and Donna whispered to me, "*That lady is rich, look at how she is dressed.*" Sure enough, Anita called out the couple and the lady was introduced as the former wife of Del Webb the former owner of the New York Yankees and her new husband who was the owner of a NBA professional basketball team. He must have been rich too but you never would have believed it based on the way he was dressed. I was especially impressed since as a kid I was an ardent Yankee fan!

Some Sundays we travelled to Branson to attend "church". Many of the theaters turned into churches on Sunday with the stars leading prayer services as well as providing free music entertainment. Several times we locals were invited to be in the audience free while a TV show was being taped. One such show we saw was hosted by John Ritter of Three's Company fame for Feed The Children. Wayne Newton performed in that one.

Sometimes we traveled to Branson to just eat or shop. Branson had a Cracker Barrel which was our favorite, and of course there were several McDonald's and other fast food restaurants. Our shopping trips usually were to several big outlet malls in the area. Donna loves to shop and this was one of her favorite activities when we visited outside the woods. I tagged along on shopping trips and spent a lot of the time in the snack bars which were there, I am sure, for husbands only.

Springfield

Springfield, MO was a large city with a population of over 168,000 people and was 90 miles from our cabin. It had many "real" chain restaurants, a Best Buy, a Barnes and Noble and large air conditioned malls. It even had a zoo.

Donna loved the zoo and visited there several times while I did something else. The Springfield Zoo had an elephant that you could ride. Once when Donna visited there she came close to riding the elephant. It only cost $15 but she didn't ride it because there was no one around to take a picture and she figured I wouldn't believe her without a picture. I never went with her but I believe her that it was a great zoo and that she "almost" rode the elephant.

We also visited a college in Springfield and used their library. I took out books that I needed for a distance education course I was taking. Sometimes we just read books and magazines there and enjoyed the air conditioning. That was nice because in the summer it can get very hot in Southern Missouri.

The second year we were in Missouri Donna and I would go to Springfield weekly when I was in training as a life insurance agent, which for me was not a pleasant experience. More of that later.

We loved the area that we lived in, but there were times we realized that to some that we didn't "fit in".

Chapter 6 - Damn Yankees

In the Civil War Missouri "kind of" stayed in the Union. It was a border state that had both Union and Confederate sympathizers. By the end of the war the Union troops outnumbered the Confederate troops three to one. During the war the Missouri government officials, including the governor, fled to the South and moved the Missouri capital to Marshall, Texas. A new Union backing government also was formed.

The Southern Missouri officials in exile voted that Missouri succeed from the Union. They sent their own Senators and Congressmen to Richmond, the capital of the Confederacy. The officials still in Missouri sent their representative to Washington. General Grant and his very big army were credited with keeping the "real" Missouri in the Union. Most citizens were conflicted.

In many ways the Civil War never ended in the South. We found this out early. A few of our neighbors considered us "Damn Yankees". After the Civil War many Northerners moved south during reconstruction to start businesses and run for office. They were called "Carpet Baggers". We were told by our "local" friends they and others didn't want Northerners to come with their ideas, but they did want our money. We even overheard a conversation in a store where someone said,

"Northerners come and Northerners go but they always leave their money."

However, mostly we were accepted by our neighbors in the woods, except for one incident that was chilling.

Almost everyone had a pickup truck and we had one too. The problem was that for several months after we moved we still had a New York license plate. Once I was approached in a store by the owner who growled, "*Are you bringing your New York way of thinking here?*" He told me in very specific terms what would happen to anyone who tried that. I rapidly left his store, jumped into the pickup truck, told Donna what he said and sped out of his parking lot, never to return.

So we did the best we could to fit in. We joined a local church and met our neighbors. We found there were many like us around from the North who were trying to "fit in" and in addition we found many friendly locals.

We eventually got a Missouri license plate for our pick up truck and new driver's licenses.

When we went to get a license plate at the county seat the clerk asked us if we wanted a local "county only" plate or a plate that would allow us to drive out of the county. At first we thought she was kidding. She wasn't! We elected for a "drive anywhere" version. This sounded strange to us but while in Missouri we did meet several people who had the "local" plates and they told us that indeed they never left the county.

With our local identification secure, we"kind of " fit in with others living in the woods. But there were other difficulties.

Chapter 7 - Rocky Roads on Highway 815

Our property was located on the crossroads of Highway 815, Highway 815 and Highway 815. Believe it or not that was our address. Highway 815 ran all over the mountain in our area but the three links ended up in front of our cabin even though you couldn't see the cabin down our lane. We used that as our address and never missed a United Parcel Service (UPS) delivery. The regular mail went to a post office box in town. We marveled at how the UPS driver found us.

One day we ordered a rental car so we could drive to see our daughter in Illinois. Our red pickup truck (our only vehicle) was getting older and we were afraid it would not make the trip. The rental car company advertised that they would deliver up to 50 miles so we requested a delivery. The poor driver of the rental car company and the driver of the follow-up car found us after driving 45 miles from Mountain Home, AR. I am sure they changed their policy of free delivery of rental vehicles within 50 miles after that experience.

That is pretty funny but there is even more. The roads from the main Highway 160 which was paved to our place, were all dirt and rocky. Actually there were many sharp big rocks on the road too. I know because the first few weeks we had three flats and the tread was shred from the rest of the tires. Before we moved to the woods, I thought we would have no problems on dirt roads since we bought expensive tires rated for off-road use, but no.

Finally, in desperation, I visited a local tire dealer to ask for his advice.. He laughed and said,

"Off road tires were made to look good but they are worthless on these roads. Off road tires work best on paved roads. City slickers just like the looks of them."

He recommended a South Korean tire made of mainly plastic. I took his advice and bought five of them. I never had a flat again. However, the downside was that driving on plastic tires on paved roads became a very bumpy experience indeed! Think of a bouncing beach ball.

Now that we had tires that would climb the mountains without shredding, we had to learn how to get up the hills without good traction. The first few times we tried to climb two real steep places on curves, the wheels just spun on the rocks and the truck stood still. We had to back up and take a very long circuitous route that added miles to the trip to our cabin.

After many unsuccessful attempts to get up the dirt road, a neighbor gave us advice how to get up the steepest parts of the dirt and rocky road. He said you had to start at a flat space on the road, get a running start and get up to a good speed. Once you got to the crossroad you had to do a maneuver that race car drivers and police use to slide the rear end around until you face the road ahead up the hill. Then you gun it again and if you are lucky you could make it to the top of the hill. After lots of practice, I got pretty good at getting home in a fairly reasonable time. So did Donna. It was an exciting adventure every time we left the woods for civilization.

Believe it or not, we did eventually get many guests to our mountain. We rarely saw other cars on our rocky roads. Some visitors didn't even complain and I am still amazed about that. We just told them our address: Intersection of Highway 815, Highway 815 and Highway 815.

However, two other stories are worth mentioning.

She Never Came Back

I remember the day that one of our first visitors pulled into our driveway. As we greeted her, I noticed she was shaking. Her face was ashen and she had difficulty talking. Once she regained her composure, she blurted, "*If I ever visit you again, I'm staying in a motel in town, and you can visit me there.*"

I was afraid to tell her there was only one motel within 45 miles from our cabin and it wasn't much to look at. She never came back.

Clyda

Donna's cousin, Clyda, lived about 50 miles from us. She was talented in decorating and one day visited to help Donna. We greeted her on the front poach and she said, "*How in the world did you ever find this place*?"

You could tell by her body language that she was concerned. She said that she never had been on roads in Missouri as bad as the roads to get to our cabin. We explained that school busses travelled twice a day on those roads and one day we even saw a county plow on the roads the one time it snowed. She just shook her head.

Clyda also never came back.

However, we adjusted to the roads and made local friends that visited us often over the two years we lived in Missouri. Our other children were braver and made it up the mountain with no complaints.

We did finally found another route to get to civilization from our cabin. We learned that if you turned right out of our lane and kept on that branch of Highway 815, rather than driving straight out of our lane onto that Branch of Highway 815, the right way continued on to a road that was still dirt but less rocky and more level than the straight way. That "right way" led to the same paved Highway 160 that we went to when took the straight way from our lane. Who knew?

The lesson is that there isn't always one "right way". I wish we had learned that lesson much earlier. Maybe our first guest and Clyda would have come back to see us if they had started from the right way, not the straight way. Are you confused yet?

Donna just reminded me of another funny story that related to Highway 815. It's about a unique vehicle that came up our lane - from the right way. :)

Chapter 8 - Did You Order a Hearse?

One day Donna called out: "*Dan, there is a hearse coming down the lane with a canoe on the roof.*" That started a friendship with our new neighbors.

The driver and his wife introduced themselves. They were from Wisconsin and were both psychologists. They were very friendly and good listeners and I would say very "unique".

They just bought the 40 acres next to our land (we could get there by turning right out of our lane onto Highway 815). They explained that they were going to build cabins to rent and set up a retreat where people could escape, for a while, to the peace and quiet of the mountains. I assumed they would provide programs to assist in the calming process.

We asked them why they had a hearse. They explained that they were able to get it at a good price and that it had low milage and was kept in great condition by the previous owner. Donna remembers that they said they liked it because it had plenty of room. As I remember, the canoe paddles were in the back and there were no seats. On one trip to their woods they brought the man's mother. She must have ridden between them in the front seat, I hope!

They travelled back and forth from Wisconsin as the cabins were built. They alway stopped to visit with us when they came. I also remember seeing them driving in the nearby small town with the canoe still on the top of the hearse. In fact, I don't remember seeing the hearse without the canoe on top.

Work on the cabins was incomplete while we lived in the mountains. We never knew where they stayed when they visited. Maybe in the hearse?

We liked that couple and enjoyed visiting with them. I still wonder what ever became of their dream for a retreat in the mountains.

However, there is more to this story. It's about trees.

Chapter 9 - Trees: More or Less

As I explained in the previous story, our hearse friends from the right way on Highway 815 were building retreat cabins in the woods. Their property was quite a distance down the road so we assumed that the construction would not affect us. That turned out to be a wrong assumption.

One day we heard the sound of chain saws. I ran down our lane to the road and saw a team of men cutting down trees along the side of the road. They were coming from the direction of the hearse couple. Our property had a road frontage of around a quarter of a mile and the trees were falling for sure on our property and the clearing was well away from the road.

I ran down to the tree cutting and found a man who looked like he was the boss. I assumed this because he wore a white helmet. I asked him what he was doing. He said,

"We are from the power company. There is no electric down the road where there is construction so we are cutting down the trees and eventually will be putting up poles and stringing power lines."

After a heated discussion, the boss agreed to saw up a portion of the fallen trees near our house up so we could use them for firewood.

As I said before, I love trees. One reason we moved to the woods was because of the trees. I loved that our 37 acres was covered with trees. Donna and I were not happy. I called the power company right away to complain but it did no good. The attack on our precious trees continued.

So sawed down trees lined the road in front of and down the road to the retreat cabin construction: the retreat that was supposed to bring people peace and calm in the woods, not so much to us. The electric poles and lines never were put in place as long as we lived on the mountain. The downed trees stayed in place except a couple that were cut up for firewood.

Now I've told about he straight way and right way at the end of our lane that both took to a branch of Highway 815. However, there is more. That is, taking a left way out our lane to another branch of Highway 815.

Chapter 10 - We Got Windows

The Shack

One day a man knocked at our door and introduced himself. He told us that he lived on Highway 815. I asked, "*Which direction*?" He answered, "*You turn left at the end of your lane.*" There was a blond Labrador Retriever in back of him. He explained it wasn't his dog, but it followed him everywhere he went and he fed it. We invited the stranger in but not the dog.

He asked us if we wanted to hear him sing his newest song. "*Sure*", I said. Then he belted out the song with a pretty good loud voice. Donna and I looked at each other in amazement. Our conversation took many directions. He was very friendly and so were we. He invited us to come over and visit him. We eventually did. I'll call our new friend Ben. I can't remember his real name.

One day I walked down Highway 815 and found the lane to Ben's house that he said led to his property. His lane was not in good condition to say the least. To say there were ruts, potholes and rocks on the dirt road would be an understatement. I had a hard time making it down the lane on foot. I couldn't image how a vehicle would make it.

Our new friend Ben lived in a partially finished shack that looked more like a lean-to with a bed. He didn't have water or electricity, but his property had plenty of trees for other things. The ground around his "home" was littered with lumber, bricks, shingles, empty water bottles and other building materials that looked like Ben found them in a dumpster.

Ben had great plans for his property. He said the only things he needed to make his shack a castle were windows. He wanted to put them on all sides of his place so he had a view of the trees.

Donna just reminded me that she went to Ben's place with me too and that it was a pitiful circumstance that he lived in.

Ben was a nice guy in my opinion, but it was evident that he was very much down on his luck. He told me his wife left him. Enough said about that. I felt sorry for him and wanted to help him with his project if I could. I walked home and told Donna Ben's sad tale. I explained that he said all he needed to complete his project were windows. Donna took note of that.

Now to a trip we took to Indiana to visit Donna's family.

The Windows

It was almost 400 miles from where we lived in Missouri to where Donna's family lived. Our red pickup truck bounced along the Interstate highways on our new plastic tires. We enjoyed our brief escape from the woods.

We visited Donna's mother and father and her sister Susie's house. It was an older house in a nice neighborhood not too far from Donna's parents. After a pleasant visit Susie proudly showed us her new windows. Donna asked her. "*Where are your old windows?*" At first I was puzzled why Donna asked that. Susie replied, "*In the garage. Do you want to see them*?"

So we trudged out to the small detached garage. Susie opened the door and we saw that the garage was almost filled with old wood framed windows. Donna asked, "*Can we have them?*" Then it stuck me that Donna wanted them so we could gift them to Ben. One thing I learned about Donna is that she is good at connecting thoughts. I am not.

I pulled our pickup truck up to the garage and started loading . I was not happy with this plan. As we loaded I notice that the pickup was getting closer to the ground. By the time we finished loading I am sure the truck was resting on it's springs.

So we headed out on the Interstate late in the afternoon. Did I say I was not happy? I kept it slow as we lumbered down the speedway, now in the dark. Then disaster struck as we drove around St. Louis!

We heard a loud "pop" and the car lurched to the right. I slowed down and pulled off to the side of the road. It was pouring. I got out and saw that we had a flat plastic tire. For sure heavy load was the cause. Donna held a flashlight in the pouring rain as I jacked up the truck and put on the spare tire. I worried that the jack would give way to the weight of Susie's old windows. Donna just reminded me that in addition to the downpour it was almost freezing cold and she worried my fingers would freeze to the metal jack handle. But we did make it back safely to the woods before sunrise.

Once we got back I was eager to unload the heavy load from the pick-up - once! So early in the morning I headed to Ben's "construction" site. I pulled into his lane bouncing along deep ruts, potholes and rocks. My hands started sweating and I could only image that the truck would get so badly damaged that it would end up as part of Ben's construction site. But I drove ever so slowly and made it to his shack.

Ben was happy to see me and very happy to finally have windows for his dream home. I was happy to get rid of the windows and even happier when I pulled out of Ben's lane onto Highway 815.

We never turned left out of our lane again and Ben never sang us another song.

Chapter 11 - Our Pets in the Woods

Before we moved to the woods, I wasn't so much of an animal lover. When I was a kid I had a pet dog, a cat and several small snapping turtles. (One day when I was a kid my cat bit the heads off the snapping turtles.) When my children were young we had a dog and several cats. When I got older, I thought pets were too much trouble. That being said, my attitude towards animals softened in the woods. We lived among the animals - we were the visitors. Here are stories about some of the true owners of the woods.

The Range Dog

One day a fairly large dog lumbered down our lane (he may have been the dog following Ben on his visit to our house). He looked like he had been in the woods a while. But he was friendly. At first we ignored him but he kept coming back, always waging his tail. We begin to look forward to his visits.

One of our neighbors told us he was a "range dog". That is, there are some dogs that are like orphans. Either they ran away from home or their owners abandoned them. Others may have been born in the woods, their mom being a range dog. We never named him.

He explained that range dogs have a territory, maybe even 50 miles, and that they roam from place to place. If they are treated well or given food they come back - the better they are treated, the more they come back.

Then I started putting out water for our range dog. I made sure I fussed over him - petted him, etc., but I never gave him a name. He did come back almost every day for a while, but then his visits came only a couple day a week.

I missed him and my heart softened. I drove to the local feed store and bought a 50 pound bag of dog food. I calculated if he got food from us he would give us a higher priority for his visits.

I put food out and the next day it was still there. After a week of no range dog I was sad. I talked to our neighbor about that. He explained, "*You missed it. He moved on the greener pastures. You'll never see him again.*" We didn't!

I learned a lesson from the range dog. If you want love, you have to love first. Maybe I should have given him a name. I can't remember what I did with the 50 pound bag of dog food.

We remembered the range dog lesson when we encountered some orphans in our wood pile.

Kittens in the Woodpile

One day I was walking next to the woodpile by our outbuilding. I heard a very soft "*Meow.*" I looked down and a very small kitten was looking up at me. When I stepped towards the kitten, it fled into the woodpile. I ran to the cabin and told Donna what happened. We went to the woodpile and quietly waited to see if a kitten would appear. It took a while, but eventually two kittens emerged. Again, as we approached, the kittens they ran into the woodpile.

This repeated for several days until there were four little kitten. Seeing no mother cat in sight, I felt sorry for them and wondered how they survived. Remembering how we lost our chance to keep the range dog around, we took a saucer of milk next to the woodpile. Eventually, one by one, the kittens came out of the woodpile and lapped at the milk. However, to our dismay, every time we came near them, they retreated to the woodpile. I told Donna, *"I would like to pet and even hold them."* Donna came up with a plan.

Every day we placed the saucer of milk a little further from the woodpile and closer to where we sat. At first the kittens would hesitate and look at us before they slowly came out to the saucer. Day by day they and the saucer came closer to us and eventually we could pet them, hold and love them.

One day we came out to the woodpile with the saucer of milk and only three kittens appeared. We never saw the forth kitten again. We assumed he or she ran into a fox or other wild animal and got eaten.

This relationship with the three kittens continued throughout our stay in the woods. It brought us great joy. They, as with the range dog, were never named, but they were loved.

The three little kittens lived in our woodpile the rest of the time we lived in the woods.

Birthday Gift Kitty

One other pet I thought that I had in addition to the woodpile kittens was one given to me by our son John and his girlfriend (now wife) Amy.

It was my birthday and John and Amy came to visit. I am not sure if their visit was timed for my birthday, but they did bring a present. They walked into the cabin with a shoebox with a bow on top. Amy called out, "*Happy Birthday!*" I was pleased because as a child I didn't get birthday presents on my birthday since it fell a few days after Christmas. At best, the card on my Christmas presents would say, "*Merry Christmas and Happy Birthday!*"

Amy carefully put the box in my outstretched arms. As she did the box began to shake. I heard scratching and the shoebox almost jumped out of my arms. "*What the heck*!", I shouted. John, Amy and Donna started laughing. When I took off the big bow, "unwrapped" my present and opened the box a small black kitten jump out. Amy said, "*His name is Schiz , short for schizophrenic.*"

I was shaken and didn't know what to say. Donna and I had a rule that pets were not allowed in our cabin. We had pets in the past and decided they were too messy and we wanted to keep our cabin pristine. I was caught in a dilemma. We had a rule about no inside pets, but Schiz was a present and you can't make a live present live outside, especially one given by such a sweet couple who remembered my birthday.

The charade went on for a while and finally Amy and John confessed that Schiz was going to go home with them and this was just a prank. I became a good sport and let the tiny cute kitty, almost gift, stay as a visiter - in the cabin!

Update: Just last week I talked with Amy about this incident. She confessed that at the time they were aware of the "no pet in our place" ban. They devised a scheme to get their new pet into our cabin. They calculated that their end-around would work. Who could refuse a gift? Also, who would be so mean to toss a kitty into the woods. Little did they know about our woodpile kittens "outside" waiting for a saucer of milk and a pet of their own.

Schiz went on to live a very long life "in" John and Amy's apartment and later house. He earned his *schizophrenic name*. As a tiny kitten his crazy antics were cute but he never outgrow them over the years. He is no longer in this world.

Over the years he always hissed at me when I passed by. He must have sensed my cold heart to inside pets.

Turkeys, Birds and Deers and Such

Our cabin had a fairly large dining room area with oversized floor to ceiling windows looking out to our very big yard. The previous owner had cleared at lease an acre out of the 37 acres for the yard. It was surrounded by an Abe Lincoln Rustic Fence. In back of the fence was a small pond. You could also see the yard and pond from the deck outside of our loft bedroom.

We often saw a variety of wildlife in the yard. We suspected the pond was an attraction created by the previous owner so he could hunt from the deck. Our realtor Don told us the previous owner was a hunter as evidenced by several tree stands in the back of our woods.

That all being said, we didn't hunt but we did enjoy observing the wildlife on our 37 acres. Often, I would get up early, pour a cup of coffee and sit at the table in the dining room to watch the animal show. Often, A rafter of turkeys would appear from the woods. The husband turkey, gobbling as he proudly strutted, led the quietly clucking ladies single file into the yard as he displayed the full fan of his tail. Fawns would come into the yard prancing and dancing like children in a schoolyard as Mom deer watched from behind the Abe Lincoln Fence, ready to call them out if trouble developed.

Donna told me she once saw a red fox come into the yard. I never saw it. There were many varieties of birds around our house too. Donna set out feeders in the front of the cabin that we could see from the dining room windows. Humming birds would come to the windows when their liquid "food" feeder needed to be refilled. One other kind of bird would come to the window and peck on it when his feeder was low on his kind of food. Donna says that once he brought another bird with him to the window (probably his wife) to introduce her to us.

We read that migrating birds somehow remember where they visited on their journeys from north to south (or visa versa) and that hummingbirds travelled thousands of miles to escape the snow and cold every year. The bird experts say that the same birds visit the same houses every year on their travels. We believed that. Only God could make something that amazing happen.

We knew armadillos were around the area but we never saw one in our yard. We were told they recently came up from Texas into Southern Missouri. Many considered them pests like mice or rats. We did see quite a few dead ones on and next to the roads. Our realtor Don warned us to never try to drive over them on the road because when a vehicle passes over them they get scared and jump up and hit the bottom of the vehicle and create quite a mess. I "kind of" felt sorry for them. We were cautioned to never pet one. I don't know why we were told that.

Of course there were many snakes around the area and our 37 acres. I tried to avoid them and never would consider them as pets. I alway thought they were weird and could never understand why some people liked them so much. I have even been told stories about churches that handle snakes in their services.

Now, I'll tell you about some toys we had in the woods.

Chapter 12 - Toys in the Woods

Like many that live in the woods we accumulated toys adults enjoy including a 28 foot Fleetwood Southwind motorhome, a Polaris All Terrain Vehicle (ATV) and a pontoon boat we kept in a marina. First I'll tell you about our motorhome.

The Motorhome

Our large 28 foot motorhome was used when we bought it. It was great looking but the salesman didn't tell us we could only use it on sunny days. We discovered that on the first excursion that we took with family members. We drove down the road merrily singing, "On the Road Again" and we were, until it started raining, outside - and inside. We quickly grabbed towels and found out that our used motorhome warranty only covered mechanical problems.

I had to learn to reseal a roof of a motorhome before we could head out again with rain in the forecast.

For a while it worked fine mechanically. However, we learned the hard way that taking care of a motorhome is a challenge, especially in the woods.

When it came time for a routine oil change we took it to the nearest Chevrolet garage. The nearest motorhome dealer was too far away. We called the garage and made an appointment and they proudly confirmed they could handle a motorhome. However, when we got to the garage we saw the building was very old and small. It probably had been built when the automobiles were started with a crank.

I'll give the garage credit though. They didn't flinch when they saw our 28 foot behemoth. One by one they drove the other vehicles out of the shop until our big boy would fit. We were happy they got the oil change done until the shop manager, red faced, told us to not come back.

Once months later the motorhome failed at the end of a trip. Fortunately, it died as we drifted back to the campground site we were on. We found that getting a tow for a motorhome was a big deal. Many hours later a tow truck appeared and off our motorhome went many miles away to the nearest repair facility.

We did take a couple of longer trips with the motorhome and found the cost of gas was great. We were lucky to get six miles to the gallon. We also found side trips difficult. For example, when we went shopping we had to unhook the motorhome and set it up again when we returned to the campsite. Many RVers solved this problem by towing a small car.

We finally stopped taking trips in the motorhome and just parked it next to our oversized out building near our cabin in the woods. Electricity was available and I rigged up a very long series of hoses for water. Thereafter, the motorhome was used as a "get-away" place for us and someplace to stay for our visitors. There was room to sleep four, a TV and sound system as well as a refrigerator and stove. There was even a furnace for winters and a bathroom for showers - and the woods for other needs. It was only used again on the road when we finally headed out of the woods to civilization. I'll tell you more about that later.

Our ATV

We bought the ATV before we moved to the woods. We used it first at a camping ranch where we were members. It was a lot of fun. There were miles and miles of dirt roads around our 37 acres and plenty of trails thru the woods on our property. When people visited they also road the ATV.

Pontoon Party on the 4th of July

Another toy was a pontoon boat we bought when we moved to the woods. It was docked in a local marina. It looked pretty good there. Before we bought it the owner let us take it on a ride on the big lake. It worked fine - at least then.

Shortly thereafter we took it out on a voyage to a local restaurant on the lake. The pontoon ran well and the food was good too. However, on our trip back the motor gave out in the middle of the lake. I couldn't get it started. I also tried to start up the battery powered auxiliary trolling motor but it was dead too. There we sat with nobody in sight and it was getting dark. Luckily, I had a cell phone and I called the marina. They came out and gave us a tow. When the guys in the tow boat pulled up, one guy asked,"*How did you contact us?*" I held up my big bag cell phone. He looked puzzled. Cell phones were not as common as they are now.

We found out the engine was shot and were directed to a local boat mechanic. He gave the motor a complete overhaul. Winter was coming and it sat in the marina for months. We didn't even try to restart it after the overhaul.

We naively believed the pontoon was ready to sail again. The first adventure after the repair was set for the 4th of July when our family was to visit. We packed picnic baskets, loaded up ice chests and drove to the marina. Everyone crammed into the pontoon, put on bright orange life jackets and waited patiently for our lake 4th of July adventure to start. So I turned the key to start the motor. It sputtered a bit and died. I tried to start the pontoon motor again and again, but to no avail. It just wouldn't start!

Undeterred, we took off our life vests, unpacked out picnic baskets and had a great 4th of July party on the water - in the marina. Anissa, the Duck Captain, climbed up in the Captain's chair of the pontoon and took the helm of the motionless ship.

That was the last "almost voyage" we took on our pontoon. We only had one "real" voyage. We sold it before we escaped the woods. I felt bad because several family members on our failed boat party were also with us on our first rainy trip in our motorhome.

For sure we were "city slickers" and in this case our money stayed on the lake. But we were undeterred, because we were "rich".

Chapter 13 - Being Rich in the Woods

I always considered myself middle class; not poor but certainly not rich. However, I found when we moved to the woods that we were "rich" - or so our neighbors thought.

Our cabin had an old heat pump. One day a few months after we moved, it's blower unit in our crawl space stopped working. We checked around and found that one of our neighbors fixed such things. We called him over. He was very pleasant but he looked and sounded like a local for sure - a heavy beard and Missouri accent. He had a pistol strapped on which made me nervous. I asked him why he wore it. "*I carry it because there are often rattle snakes under these cabins and I don't want to get bit.*" He ended up putting a new unit in the crawl space and our heat pump was back in good shape.

We eventually became friends with the furnace guy and his family. They lived about a mile down the road - our nearest neighbors. To my surprise, I found out that they had moved to Missouri from Illinois in a city only 35 miles away from where we lived. I also found out he had been a deputy sheriff. (That explained the gun.)

The furnace guy eventually told us that we were considered "rich" by the locals because we had a septic tank. He explained that many people up on our mountain simply had their waste water piped "down the hill". I am not sure he was serious, but the more I knew of the area, the more I believed him

Following is another story about how being "rich" can cost you money.

Chapter 14 - The Auction and a Lesson

My son Rob was in college and had an old car that was giving him trouble. He was visiting us in the woods. I heard about a car auction in the next county and thought that I might be able to get a good deal on a better vehicle for him there. He told me he wanted a small pick-up truck. So a plan developed for us to go to the auction looking for a small pick-up truck for a bargain. I was going to pay for it but my limit would be $2000.

A friend who was local warned me to be careful buying at that auction. He told me, "*Those good old boys over there know a city slicker when they see one.*" He recommended that we not go over there.

I thought I could out-smart anyone in the back country being an East Coast college graduate. Boy was I wrong. This is what happened.

Rob and I drove over to the auction. One by one the cars started rolling into a huge building where Rob and I waited. The auctioneer started the auction. We had a card with a number on it. Finally a real cute red small pick-up rolled by. A couple of men were on both sides.

Rob said, "*This is the one Dad. I love it.*" The bidding started low and the bidding kept going until I bid $750.00 and the bidding stopped. The auctioneer yelled out, "*Sold*". I paid for the truck at the front of the building and Rob's "new" truck was waiting for us outside the door. We didn't pay attention how it got there,

Rob jumped in and checked things out. Then he called out, "*Dad, the radio has been taken out.*" We inspected the tires and found the tread was almost worn off. That was the least of what we found out wrong about the "bargain" truck.

It barely started. The muffler rumbled, the wheels wobbled and the engine rattled along; but we did make it back to the cabin. I had a sick feeling that I had been taken as my friend had warned. I even suspected that the men that walked the truck into the auction may have pushed it so the engine rattling would not be heard.

Undeterred, I told Rob we would take it to the local garage that had been doing my oil changes. The shop was in an old gas station, the kind I remembered from the 1950s.

So we took it over to the garage and waited while the mechanic checked it out. Finally, he slowed waked up to us with a troubled look on his face. "*Where did you get this?*" Then he started listing what "had" to be done to get it back to Rob's town. Then he listed what was needed to keep it running beyond a couple of weeks. The numbers rose as he spoke. I gasped. The total far exceeded my budget, so I settled for repairs to get it back to Rob's town.

Rob left his old clunker in our barn and headed north full of youthful optimism in his "new" red pick-up truck. I was too embarrassed to tell my local friend the end of the story and he never asked.

I learned a couple of months later from Rob that his truck broke down shortly after he made it home and a mechanic there told him the cost to fix it which Rob couldn't afford. Rob traded the truck in on a brand new small car that was left over from previous years because of its awful color. It was pink. He never told me how much he got on a trade-in but I believe he may have had to pay to have it towed to the garage and they junked it.

The moral of the story is to never think you can outsmart locals. That lesson cost me almost $2000.

In the years we lived in the woods, Rob was our most frequent visiter. Following is a story about one of his special visits.

Chapter 15 - The Big Christmas Tree

At the back of our 37 acres, there was a stand of evergreen trees. Many of these trees were the perfect size to be a Christmas tree. So in early December we would drive our 4-wheeler to where the trees were and cut down a tree and take it back to the cabin to decorate.

One year Rob came to visit at Christmastime. In the previous year we cut down and decorated a "normal" size tree. Donna settled for the "normal" tree but really wanted a "real" big tree. The reason being that our cabin had a "real" high ceiling that could only be reached by a "real" high ladder.

So Rob and I took the ATV down the lane to the back of our property where there was a stand of "Christmas" trees. It didn't take us long to find the tallest and best looking one. We cut it down and dragged it to back to the cabin. Donna, Rob and I set it up and decorated it. Rob could not stay for Christmas but we were sure appreciated his help to make a wonderful memory.

Local friends came over for a Christmas party that year. The fellowship and prayer were special. That Christmas was the only one in the woods. Next year we travelled to Illinois for Christmas with Amanda and family.

Eventually I looked for a job to supplement our income.

Chapter 16 - My First Job in the Woods.

We planned to live in the woods using our retirement savings. After a while we found we needed more money to live. I took some teaching courses in college and back East I did some substitute teaching. So I drove to a local school and applied for a job as a substitute teacher. The school had students from kindergarten to 12th grade.

I went into the Principal's office, told the secretary I was applying for a job as a substitute teacher and filled out an application. I headed for the our pickup truck in the parking lot. All of the sudden the principal came running after me and offered me a job on the spot. It seems that the 6th-8th grades history teacher had just notified him she was pregnant and needed a leave. It turned out that I took her classes for 8 weeks.

The teacher met with me once. She handed me the school books for each class as well as copies of past tests and outlines of lesson plans. However, she said that I could just create the lesson plans and tests myself if I wanted. I only had a few days to prepare,

Most of the time I prepared the lesson plans the day before the classes. However, I did follow the textbooks. They were actually pretty good since they were older and were in my view more accurate than newer textbooks. For example, they said that Columbus Discovered America and how the United State was founded on Christian principles. The Gideons were allowed to come into school and pass out Bibles that could be kept in the classrooms. Times have changed!

I was paid $35.00 a day plus all the food I could eat in the cafeteria for breakfast and lunch. I got to like hot dogs and french toast sticks like we used to have in the 1950s.

Of course, I was also on duty in the cafeteria with the other teachers to keep some sort of order during the meals. We teachers sat at the front of the lunchroom and ate together. There was a TV on the table facing the students. A video played showing students sitting in a bus. It was done to show the kids that what they did on the busses was monitored and that they had better be good. What the kids didn't know was that the school only had one camera and recorder and they moved it around from bus to bus.

The kids were mostly well mannered. If anyone acted up you could send them to the principals office and he had paddle that he could use. I'm not sure if he ever did, but the kids would behave if you threatened to send them to see the principal.

I enjoyed the experience and was sad when the real teacher came back and I had to leave. The 6th grade kids even held a surprise going away party for me in the gym. The principal led me blind folded into the gym and I teared up when I saw the smiling faces of kids. The party was very special to me since the sixth grade gave me the hardest time.

That was a great experience. I kept my name on the list of substitute teachers and I would fill in occasionally the whole time we were in Missouri but never more than a couple of days at a time. However, we needed more money. Eventually I looked for a better paying job. That takes me to my next story that tells a colorful tale.

Chapter 17 - Turning Orange in the Woods

The first year in the woods was exciting and fun. I enjoyed my substitute teaching experience. The second year was not so exciting and fun. I started missing my life outside the woods. I missed my friends, my family and I guess just civilization. The nearest McDonald's was around 50 miles away as I explained before. A mall was 90 miles away. The population of the nearest town was around 300.

I started staying in the cabin more. We had satellite TV installed and I spent many hours watching TV, eating cheese curls and drinking Diet Pepsi. I tossed the empty Pepsi bottles in the bed of our pick-up truck and drove to the recycle center when it filled - which was often. I also gradually turned orange from the cheese curls and gained over 50 pounds.

Donna, on the other hand, headed into the woods most days. Sometimes she stayed out of the cabin until dusk. I don't blame her considering my pathetic condition. She cleared brush and moved rocks around. I seldom followed her.

Finally I woke from my despair. (That's another story I may tell someday in another book.) The fog cleared and I decided to use my insurance credentials and applied for a job as a life insurance agent and registered representative (selling mutual fund and variable annuities) for a big life insurance company.Following is a story about that.

Chapter 18 - Looking for $$$ in the Woods

The school offered me a job as a half-time computer teacher. They had a federal grant for that job. The pay was $6000 for the school year. I almost took it until I found out they wanted me to teach for a full day (at a half day pay) and there were no benefits except breakfast and lunch. I seriously considered taking it.

In my corporate career I took many insurance and finance classes and held several professional designations. I had enough courses in economics in college for a minor in economics. It was natural for me to seek a job as life insurance salesman, so I did.

I got a job with a top life insurance company and became licensed to sell life insurance as well as other financial investments such as mutual funds. In my training period Donna and I travelled to Springfield which was 90 miles away once a week. Donna shopped while I attended meetings, took classes and made "cold calls". Once Donna almost road an elephant! (See Chapter 5)

The office had a room set up with small tables. Each had a phone and a phone book. We spent several hours calling phone numbers one-by-one. Most people hung up when I said I worked for a life insurance company. Older people were often confused and were polite and talked longer but most of this group also hung up eventually. For every hundred calls, four or five people would listen. If you were lucky two or three would agree to meet to discuss life insurance.

I didn't like the rejection. However, we were taught that success was a numbers game. Most phone contacts would not pan out so you had to call hundreds of people every day to be successful. After you met with people, if you knew what you were doing, you could expect 2 or 3 sales a week.

My manger showed me that you would become "rich" if you could keep up this pace. I was so excited about making big money that I jumped into the program. I took classes in how to handle objections, how to close a sale and how to network. We even were told to look though newspapers to get ideas for prospects. He told about one agent who would get the names of lottery winners and contact them to sell annuities or life insurance.

Other tips included checking newspapers for birth notices and contacting the parents to sell a "college policy". That is, a whole life policy that would have cash value when the baby was ready to go to college. The policy could also be signed over to the graduate. One agent even had special baby gifts that he gave when he delivered the policy. Another agent checked the papers for college graduates or those getting a promotion at work and contact them abut life insurance or other investments like mutual funds that we sold.

My manager travelled a couple of times a month to our area and showed me how to network. We sat in coffee shops and met people. The key was to establish a relationship before you tried to sell. He encouraged me to join the local Lions Club and meet people who might be "prospects". I did all of these things.

He also told us that, "*There is money in the hills.*" Once he told me there was a rumor that Charles Schwab had a mansion on the lake. I would drive around the nicer neighborhood looking for mansions. I would inquire in the coffee shop if anyone knew about "a millionaire". I never turned him up (or any other millionaire for that matter). In any case I wasn't sure what I would do with him if I found him.

I lasted one year selling life insurance. My first problem was that everyone I met, I saw as a prospect. Even relatives became prospects. The first thing we had to do in training was make a list of all our relatives and friends and start contacting them. I even became a prospect because my manager wanted me to replace my investments, like mutual funds into their products. I hated this.

My second problem was that I had a conscience. One thing I was told that if someone wants to buy, sell! (As long as you are following the the law.) Two examples come to mind. One lady I called on wanted to buy a whole life insurance policy to help pay for her daughter's college. I asked, "*How much do you have saved now*?" She said, "*One $25 Savings Bond that I bought last year.*" Next, I asked how old her daughter was and she said, "*Sixteen*". I was taken aback.

I explained that the bond probably wouldn't even be worth $20 when her daughter started college. I also told her that my commission would take a good part of the first year premium and the accumulation of cash value would probably only be worth a couple of hundred dollars when her daughter was ready for college. I told her that life insurance is good for college when you buy it for a baby and the cash value builds over the years. My only advice was for her buy a term life insurance policy on her own life and make the daughter the beneficiary. She had a sad look and didn't buy either policy. I hope some other life insurance agent didn't sell her the wrong policy.

Another lady near retirement age was referred to me about buying mutual funds. She wanted me to sell her one of our company's funds to replace a fund she owned. Her fund was worth about $13,000. She was very proud that she had managed to save enough to buy that fund, but she wanted to buy a better mutual fund that would earn more money. I looked up the ratings of her fund in Morningstar and found that her funds were rated about the same as ours in the same category. I told her that I would get a commission on the sale that would reduce the number of shares she would purchase. I recommended that she hold her mutual fund.

I never changed my approach. I wanted to sleep at night.

And so it went. Donna and my relatives were my best clients. I had to have 25 sales in the first six months to keep my job and our health insurance. I was a couple of policies short near the end of the period and I "sold" Donna two more policies to save my job.

After another six more months of frustration for me and my boss, I gave up and quit sales. God Bless those who make money selling life insurance or anything else. I learned a valuable lesson.

Chapter 19 - Baby in the Woods

Our daughter Amanda and our first granddaughter Anissa lived in Illinois almost 500 miles away from us. (You will find stories about Anissa throughout this book.) Amanda, God Bless her, wanted Anissa to be a part of our life. So she drove Anissa halfway to our home in Missouri several times and we met her and took Anissa back to our cabin. Anissa's visits were pure joy.

Anissa loved to "drive" our motorhome and 4 wheeler. (Both pictures here were staged.) She also loved to hike around our 37 acres and play with the kittens who had adopted us. (The ones that came out of our woodpile.)

We took her with us when we shopped and one time we took her to our favorite restaurant by the local marina. Our one and only trip there was memorable. We ordered full meals for ourselves and Anissa's favorite - macaroni and cheese. Before we took a bite she started howling. We couldn't comfort her. So we sheepishly had the waitress box up our uneaten meals and hurriedly we left for home.

Anissa's visits were special.

Chapter 20 - Faith in the Woods

Perhaps the most life-changing experiences I had in the woods were meeting people with great faith.

One of the main reasons we moved to Missouri was so I could help a local ministry with its publications. I met the leader, Dan, at a Christian men's group in New York. He moved his ministry to Missouri near where we used to vacation and where we decided to move.

We attended a Bible study at Dan and his wife Ruth's house weekly and met several local people that way. The Bible study was simple. We always had coffee or tea and Ruth alway provided some scrumptious sweet. We and the others always felt loved and welcome. We read the scriptures, discussed them and always ended in prayer. Dan and Ruth's quiet faith helped build my faith.

Church in a Warehouse

One church we attended met in an old tire warehouse. We met the pastor Bob and his family years before at a camping resort we belonged to. They were great people. He led a weekly church service there. Eventually he quit the campground church and started the tire warehouse church.

Part of the roof of the warehouse had caved in and the rest of the building was not in much better shape. The seats came from an old movie theatre. Some were attached by rows and others just wobbled when you sat in them. An old window air conditioner was set over the front door. The first time we came in this church drops of water splashed on our heads from the air conditioner. Bob greeted us and said,

"Welcome to our church. We baptize people here as they come in!"

We heard some of the best sermons that I have ever heard in that church.Bob's wife Lola and the rest of the family provided wonderful Southern Gospel music. One time Bob gave a great "old fashioned" Bible based sermon. His mother jumped up and yelled out, "*Bob, I haven't heard preaching like that since I was a little girl.*"

When Bob's mother passed, the church met in a graveyard for a celebration of her life. There were tears of joy. She laid in a white casket as her family sang her favorite Gospel song, "Twelve Gates to the City". I'll never forget that day.

Bob, his family and the other members of his church were not rich in earthly ways but they were rich in uncommon faith. For example, Bob and Lola did not even have a furnace in their house. When it got cold they would open up the gas oven to heat the house. Many in the church did not have health insurance. When someone got sick they would call other members of the church for prayer. One time Bob had a heart attack and Lola called church members for prayer. My faith grew in that church.

Church in a Theatre

Another church we attended met in an old Branson type theater in the small town by us. Again, the preaching was excellent and Bible-based. We became friends with the pastor John and his wife Ada. We volunteered in the food pantry there where poor people would come to get food and clothing. They had to sit in the sanctuary and listen to a sermon before they were given food and chose needed clothing.

The church buildings were not fancy and most of the people who worshiped there were not rich. However, I learned that the church members were kind and generous and had great faith in God rather than in material possessions.

Chapter 21 - You Can Go Home Again

As you can tell from the above stories, our time in the woods was not all idyllic. There were many moments of joy - especially for Donna, but there were also moments of frustration and unhappiness - especially for me. I thrived on being around people. In Illinois, I was active in politics and had a good paying job. During that time I got a masters degree and completed three of the most noteworthy insurance designations. I also was elected to the County Board. But most important, I had many good friends. Moving to the woods took me away from all that.

The day came when I wanted to go home, not to my childhood home, but to Illinois where I spent most of my life. I called an executive friend at my former company and literally begged to come back. He said he would see what he could do. I wasn't an executive in the company but I did have several positions that paid very well.

After a few days he called me with bad news. There was nothing for me. My skills were stale after four years away. The new technology had passed me by. The tech world was for the young and bright who knew how to manipulate the internet and cell phone computers that were faster and smarter than humans.

However, My executive friend did offer some hope.

"The company is installing some new computer programs countrywide and we are hiring temporary workers to train non-technical people in their usage. I can arrange an interview with the temp company and you can take it from there."

I was desperate and jumped at the opportunity. We travelled to Illinois and after a very positive interview with the temp company, I got the job. The pay was half of what I made in the company six years before with few benefits. But I was very happy. Donna was very happy among the rocks and trees in Missouri and resisted at first, but finally gave in. I asked her if she would go with me if I took the job. She said, *"I think I have to, I am your wife."*

There was one loose end we needed to take care of - the woodpile kittens. We couldn't bare to leave them stranded in the woods. Donna feared they would be eaten by wild animals. So we thought of a friend from church who loved animals - especially the rescue kind.Sh agreed to take them and add them to her menagerie. We boxed them up and took them to her small home in the woods. She said they would be outside kittens because she had an indoor cat that would not welcome them, but she would be sure that they were fed and she would love on them. We left her with money to buy food for her outcasts.

A few weeks after that, we drove our motorhome out of the woods for the last time and headed back to Illinois. Eventually our cabin and the toys we had accumulated sold. We lived in the motorhome in a trailer park for a couple of months until snow started flying. We finally bought a house again and started a new phase of our life.

I learned a new lesson, "You *can go home again!*"

Chapter 22 - Conclusion: A New Life

We ended up where Donna and I started our life together as a couple. Eventually I was able to get back with my old company with a permanent job and reconnect with old friends. "Our town" had almost everything that we left in the mountains, except beautiful views and many new friends. Our old town had a Barnes and Noble and a Starbucks. I had to start again in the company in the calling center at a third of the salary I was making previously at the company. Donna stayed retired. The next 22 years were very good. We built many new memories. Our blended marriage with six children grew by adding nine more grandchildren and recently one great grandchild, Elijah, who is the son of Anissa our first grandchild.

Epilogue

Just before the coronavirus pandemic started in February 2020, I put this book aside. It was almost finished. I had been sharing chapters of the book with members of a writing group Donna and I attended. Most members did not like my writing style. (I had problems with active and passive voice among other things.) I became discouraged and finally I quit the group and stopped writing.

In the past, I wrote and published several books without the aide of a writing group. I developed my own style and thought the books were pretty good. They came from my heart. Donna was my editor, critic and encourager - best of all she was my wife from corporate life, into the woods and out of the woods. She knew the stories. I confess that I never sold great numbers of books and that I don't take criticism well. Probably because my parents spoiled me. My mom even told me I was a genius.

As I write this the world is in trouble. The pandemic has killed over a million worldwide, shut down businesses, destroyed jobs and caused us to be fearful. Government tells us we must wear masks, stop going to sports events and sit in churches built for thousands with as few as 10 others.

Add to all that, there is rioting in the cities, fires in the great forests of the West, floods, hurricanes, tornadoes and a country divided over a presidential campaign. The saddest thing is that many families are also divided. I remember the days many years ago in my hometown in Pennsylvania of heated political discussions at Thanksgiving dinner. At the end of the day, we put aside our differences and continued as a loving family. Fresh out of college, I was a liberal but years later became a conservative. My grandmother once mused, "W*e are as thick as thieves.*!" It was so true!

September 26, 2020 hundreds of thousands flocked to Washington, DC to pray for our country. Many think it would take a miracle to save our country. I agree. Many do not believe in miracles and God. I do. I do because I have seen God work. Therefore, I am optimistic about the future.

Looking back, at our move to the woods, I see many miracles. This knowledge gives me hope for our country and the world - if we return back to God.

Earlier this week we travelled to visit our daughter and family in Illinois where we once lived. It was a joyous time. A highlight was being with our first great grandchild named Elijah - another miracle. While there I decided to pick up where I left off and finish this book.

The turning point for me was when I held Elijah and he kept looking at me with keen interest. Donna told me that he wanted to know me! I knew that there was hope for the future and I decided to finish this book so he will know more of me someday.

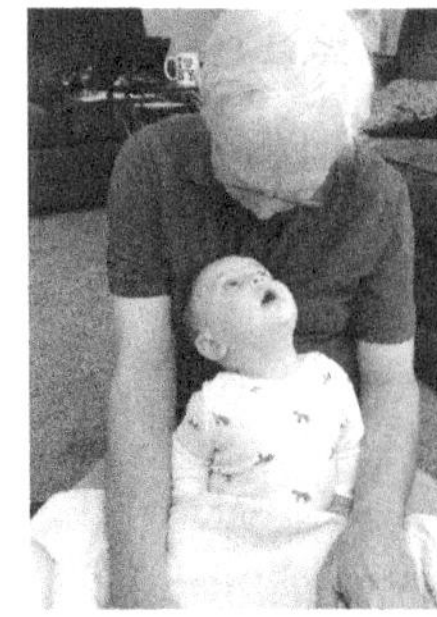

This time I am writing for myself, Elijah and anyone else who wants to know my story about how and why we moved to and from the woods. Of course there is more to my story but I'll save it for future books, God willing.

In summary, it was all good.

"And we know that in all things God works for the good of those who love Him, who have been called according to His purpose." Romans 8:28 NIV

DONNA LOVES THE WOODS

ABOUT THE AUTHOR

Dan England was born in Pennsylvania and graduated from Penn State (BA) and Illinois State (MS). Both degrees are in Political Science. He worked 34 years for a large insurance company and has written several books. Dan recently started playing in a community band the exact same alto saxophones he played in grade and high school.

Dan is married to Donna England and they have a blended family of six children, ten grandchildren and one great grandson. They are blessed.

Dan and Donna have moved to the mountains, again: This time on the plateau in Tennessee. Both are followers of Jesus. Their books can be found on Amazon.com and LuLu.-com. For questions, contact them at GCPress@aol.com.

Made in the USA
Columbia, SC
27 February 2024

32109995R00055